TOILES DE JOUY

JUDITH STRAETEN
ARCHIVIST, BRUNSCHWIG & FILS

Gibbs Smith, Publisher
Salt Lake City

First Edition
06 05 04 03 02   5 4 3 2 1

Published by

Gibbs Smith, Publisher

P.O. Box 667

Layton, Utah 84041

Orders: 1.800.748.5439

www.gibbs-smith.com

Edited by Madge Baird

Designed by Axiom Designed Communications

Special thanks to Mélanie Riffel for research

assistance in France.

Printed and bound in Hong Kong

Library of Congress

Cataloging-in-Publication Data

Straeten, Judith.

  Toiles de jouy / Judith Straeten.—1st ed.

    p. cm.

  ISBN 1-58685-156-X

    1. Calico-printing—France. 2. Textile design—
France. I. Title.

  TP930 .S934 2002

  747'.5—dc21

                  2002005185

CONTENTS

A FABRIC FOR ALL SEASONS

To the sea of pale neutrals washing over modern interiors, and the stark black that robes their inhabitants, toiles offer a stylish and increasingly popular counterpoint. Just as a black-on-white toile blazer, tote bag, or pair of slacks presents a crisp finish to an ensemble, so does toile present a range of possibilities in decorating. It can clothe an entire room—walls, curtains and upholstery—in the French provincial manner, or provide an accent in the form of cushions, lampshades or a single chair. It can be masculine or feminine, depending on the choice of color and design, and appears with equal charm in a sophisticated or casual setting. The sleek finishes of Biedermeier, the chalky pastels of country French, or the gently worn surfaces of American cottage furniture can all be used with toile.

Adults and children alike are delighted by toile's storylike patterns. These monochromatic scenic designs that seem now to be everywhere have a long lineage and, with their three- and four-color block-printed counterparts, are an integral part of the fascinating history of printed fabrics, as shown in these reprinted classic designs from *Toiles de Jouy* (pronounced twälz-da-'zhwee), an early-nineteenth-century book of samples.

Toile de Jouy has come into its own in the mainstream. And why not? Toile is elegant yet casual, rich in history yet contemporary in design, and suitable for all occasions and seemingly many décors. And we see that, after all, toile comes in more colors than blue, red, violet and black. In fact, these classic patterns show us that the origin of toile is far broader than our simple one-color understanding.

A reference today to toile de Jouy is generally understood to mean a finely detailed design with figures or flowers, usually monochromatic. This is quite different from the original meaning, which refers simply to the cloth—or *toile* in French—produced by Christophe-Philippe Oberkampf at his factory in Jouy, France. Jouy is so closely associated with the copperplate- and roller-printed fabrics that designs originally produced in Ireland, England, Germany and Switzerland by these methods, as well as by other French printing centers, are routinely characterized as "toile de Jouy."

Background

Painted and printed cottons from India were introduced into Europe early in the seventeenth century as a by-product of the spice trade. They had a profound impact on fabric design there. Prior to this, patterned fabrics were either woven or embroidered, and while printed fabrics were not entirely unheard of, they were restricted in color and were non-washable since the chemistry required to produce a colorfast printed fabric was unknown in Europe. The brilliantly colored and intricately patterned cottons from India were not only washable but also far less expensive than a woven patterned fabric. The Indian fabrics were eagerly taken up for use both in furnishings and wearing apparel.

The influence of Indian chintzes is apparent in the arrangement of many designs and in the inclusion of imaginary or fantastic flowers and creatures. But during the course of the seventeenth century, the spikey foliage and exotic blooms typical of Indian designs were modified by more familiar flowers and patterns taken from European silks and embroideries, brought to India by enterprising merchants who also organized their production for the European market.

Equally enterprising travelers sought to discover the materials and techniques used by Indian craftsmen in order to set up a printing industry in Europe, with the result that printed cottons were being produced by the 1660s in Marseille and by the 1670s in England. The popularity of printed cottons threatened to overwhelm the established silk- and wool-weaving industries of France and England within a century of their introduction, and their governments responded. In England, the importation of chintz was banned in 1700, and when this had little effect on either popularity or demand, the use of printed cottons, both imported and domestically produced, was prohibited in 1720. To protect its silk-weaving industry, France forbade both importation and production of printed cottons in 1686, a ban modified in 1752 to allow resist printing (a process of masking areas that are not to receive the dye), and finally revoked in 1756.

In neither country did these laws have the desired effect: imported Indian goods were smuggled in from Holland, and the printing industry swiftly developed in Mulhouse (not then a part of France), Switzerland and Germany.

International Influences

Woven fabrics were also sources of inspiration: the small, stylized floral motifs from the fashionable Kashmir shawls were printed to simulate woven fabrics, as were the designs of chine silks—or "clouded silks," as they were known in England—which were produced by an expensive combination of printing and weaving that imparted a characteristic blurred outline to the motifs. Floral stripes and allover floral patterns were also inspired by those of brocaded silks popular at the time. Later, a great number of patterns were based on the wealth of botanical drawings produced in the late eighteenth century.

China was another major influence on design. Chinese porcelains had been avidly collected since their first introduction into Europe. Chinese silks, painted or embroidered with delicate flowers or fantastic creatures or birds in Oriental gardens, were fashioned into gowns, furniture upholstery or wall covers for entire rooms. These products provided glimpses of a fabulous civilization intriguingly different from that of Europe, but one to which access was restricted not only by distance but also by the Chinese themselves. Travelers' descriptions and drawings of the customs, architecture and landscape of China only served to increase the allure and prompted artists such as François Boucher or Jean-Baptiste Pillement (Lyon, 1727–1808) to produce charmingly imagined scenes of Chinese life. The influence of Pillement's engravings, produced between 1755 and 1760, is discernible in a number of Jouy designs: block prints and toiles incorporate figures and florals based on his images of Oriental people and fantastic plants.

The artistic vocabulary of the designers also included the neoclassical: decorative motifs of ancient Rome such as cartouches, swags, garlands, volutes and arabesque arrangements had increasingly influenced European decorative art since the discovery of Herculaneum in 1711 and Pompeii in 1748. These were employed not only as individual elements but as framework by which vignettes, figures, vases or bouquets of flowers could be linked and framed in garlands, swags and volutes in both complex and pleasing compositions.

Oberkampf's Factory at Jouy-en-Josas

Christophe-Philippe Oberkampf (1738–1815), a Bavarian by birth, came from a family of fabric dyers and had learned the techniques of block-printing in Mulhouse and Basel before working briefly in Paris. In 1760 he set up a factory in Jouy-en-Josas, south of Paris, to take advantage of the water of the Bièvre River: printing fabric required considerable quantities of water, and Bièvre was esteemed for the purity of its water. The site had a further advantage in its proximity to the court at Versailles.

Though best known today for his plate- and roller-printed fabrics, Oberkampf's reputation in his own time was founded on the production of "indiennes," fabrics with popular multicolor block-printed patterns. Most of the designs were the small floral patterns and borders used for furnishings and popular in women's gowns and kerchiefs; men's frock coats, vests and dressing gowns; and handkerchiefs for both men and women. In fact, Oberkampf did not produce a single toile—that is, a plate-print—until the 1770s. The carefully kept records of the company's designs and production were later dispersed after it closed, but as closely as can be estimated, its block-printed patterns numbered roughly 30,000, compared to about 700 designs for plate- and roller-printing.

The names of only a few of Oberkampf's block-print designers are known today. Pierre-Guillaume Lemeunnie, also an engraver and known as Monsieur Peter, and Ludwig Rothrdorf, known as Monsieur Louis, were among the full-time staff members who produced the variety of designs. The artist responsible for a great number of the Jouy toiles is Jean-Baptiste Huet (1745–1811), a French painter who was first commissioned by Oberkampf in 1783 to create a toile cartoon celebrating the designation of the factory at Jouy as a royal manufactory (see plate 6). His depiction of the details of block-printing and plate-printing continues to delight historians and more casual viewers alike. It was followed by numerous other toiles, and he remained the major designer at Jouy until the end of his life.

After Huet's death, only a few toiles can be attributed to specific artists, among them Hippolyte Le Bas, an architect who was, appropriately, responsible for "Monuments of Paris,"and Horace Vernet, who designed "Hunting at Jouy" and was known for his paintings of Napoleonic battle scenes.

The Fabric-Printing Process

Once Oberkampf approved the designs, wood blocks were carved for printing. A separate block, roughly ten inches in each direction, was required for each color in the design, and was comprised of several layers of wood, each one about one-half inch to one inch thick, glued together with grains alternating for strength, much as plywood is today. Thin brass strips could be pounded into the block for portions of the design such as stems that would be too delicate if carved from wood. Grounds (backgrounds) could be varied by adding a layer of felt to produce a solid area of color, or by inserting small brass pins to form a dotted ground, or picotage. A pair of heavier, curved brass pins were attached, usually at the top or front of the block, to allow the printer to align each successive block with the preceding ones to properly register the different colors and produce a completed design.

Printing was done on a long table, with the surface padded to provide maximal absorption. The printer worked his way down the fabric, applying the block for each color in sequence as an assistant re-coated the block for the next application. Block-print designs at this time were actually produced by the printer applying mordants—different metallic oxides with slight color added to enable one to see the design—not the pigments themselves. These would produce various colors and bind with the cloth when immersed in a dye bath. The printed cloth was dried for several days before being soaked in a mixture of cow dung and water to remove excess mordants, then put into a boiling dye bath. Depending on the mordants used, a madder bath (made from the root of the madder plant) could produce reds, pinks, purples and lavenders, black and shades of brown; a weld bath would produce yellows and olive shades.

Indigo, for blues or layered on yellow to produce green, required a different process. (A true green was not developed at Jouy until 1806.) Since indigo does not react with mordants, it could be added by brush or with a resist dyeing process that involved masking any areas that were not to become blue. The result was a length of cloth patterned in various colors on a colored ground; to remove the unwanted ground color, the cloth was laid out in a meadow for several days, then immersed again in the dung bath and bleached. Each stage was punctuated by washing and drying; hence, the importance of a source of clean water in large quantities. The final processes were calendering—applying a mixture of starch and wax, then passing the cloth through a series of rollers to smooth the cloth—and polishing with a smooth agate to produce a glossy finish.

The fact that each of these stages—in addition to the preparation of the raw cloth and storage of raw materials, wood blocks and finished fabric—took place at Jouy explains the number and size of buildings depicted in Huet's design showing the factory (page 19). Most of the processes shown by Huet in the open were, in fact, housed in one of the buildings.

Oberkampf was known for his quality. He used the best raw materials to produce dyes and the finest grade cotton fabrics available to ensure even printing. Throughout his life he also experimented with dyes and new methods of printing, traveling extensively to other printing centers to investigate their methods. In 1769, for example, he visited the English printworks of Robert Jones at Old Ford, a printer known for his plate-printed fabric.

Intent on adding to the abilities of the factory, Oberkampf installed plate-printing equipment at Jouy in 1770. As in block-printing, the colors of toile were produced by a mordant dyeing process, but the mordant-coated plate itself remained stationary, laid face up, while cloth was pressed down on it—a reverse of the block-printing method.

The size of the plates—about 45 x 27 $\frac{1}{2}$ inches—allowed a design with a much larger repeat than that of block prints. In addition, the engraving process (which could take up to six months for a single plate) permitted such a wealth of fine detail that scenes could be depicted with a painterly attention to individual features. Together, these two characteristics of toiles provided an ideal field for illustrating multiple facets of a variety of subjects, and that remains one of their charms. Eighteenth-century toiles are typically open, composed of a series of peopled "islands" spread with airy precision across the ground and linked by smaller scenes, foliage or garlands that draw the eye from one vignette to the next.

Roller-printing was not really a new idea in the late eighteenth century: a system of wooden rollers was described in about 1701, and a workable machine using engraved copper rollers was developed in 1783 by Thomas Bell; however, due to various difficulties, the process was not used at Jouy until 1797. Oberkampf's nephew, Samuel Widmer, developed not only a workable machine but also a method of engraving the cylinders in five or six days.

The advantage was obvious: it provided continuous printing that vastly increased production. On the other hand, the circumference of the roller, which dictated the size of the repeat, was much less than that of the plate—roughly fourteen to twenty inches—and this led to a major stylistic change from open airy compositions to more compact ones. Rather than complex painterly scenes arranged in graceful rhythms to be read at the will of the viewer, early-nineteenth-century toiles more frequently offer a series of framed figures or motifs set out with geometric precision, and a strong horizontal or vertical emphasis, often against a patterned ground. Classical or mythological themes became increasingly popular, although other categories were represented as well.

After Oberkampf's death in 1815, the factory continued production under the direction of his son Emile until 1822, when he retired for reasons of health. He was followed by partner Jacques-Juste Barbet, who continued Oberkampf's tradition of innovation. But tastes were changing, and the fortunes of the factory declined until it was finally closed in 1843. Unfortunately, all records of the designs and production were dispersed when the property was sold at auction, so we must depend on careful detective work and the chance survival of information for our knowledge of the factory that produced so many designs that still beguile us today.

The Stories

The medium of toile was ideal for telling stories, and certainly they abound: the legends of Robinson Crusoe, Paul et Virginie, the Fables of La Fontaine and Don Quixote were taken from literature. There were also toiles based on plays that were popular at the time. These are among the most difficult to decipher today, as the plots are often no longer familiar. Chinoiserie toiles depicted life as imagined in China, replete with pagodas, oriental gardens, junks, strangely eroded rocks and figures in palanquins (enclosed litters carried on men's shoulders).

Toiles with historical themes show scenes from the lives of Joan of Arc, Mary Queen of Scots or Henri IV of France. Those based on then current events include "Monuments of Egypt" (inspired by Napoleon's expedition), or the still-popular "Balloon of Gonesse." Toiles with scenes from Greek and Roman mythology, which include gods, goddesses and their attributes, make up a large category, as might be expected in an age when a classical education was considered necessary for a gentleman. Hunting toiles depict one of the nobility's favorite occupations.

But the largest group—the one with the most captivating scenes—is that referred to as genre scenes, or pastorals. These provide romantic views of the pleasanter aspects of country life, reflecting the beliefs of Jean-Jacques Rousseau and the court of Marie Antoinette. The scale of the repeat in these designs made them unlikely choices for apparel, but they were ideal for furnishings. The late-eighteenth-century French taste for covering an entire room en suite in a single toile pattern retains its charms today.

Toile de Jouy Today

Many of the toiles and block-printed patterns produced at Jouy, as well as those produced in other printing centers in France, England, Germany and Switzerland, are still available. Few are still produced, however, by the original methods. Charles Burger continues to print toiles in the original narrow widths with copper rollers. Available through Quadrille, these include a number of the favorite eighteenth-century Jouy patterns such as "Balloon de Gonesse" and "La Bastille" (also known as "Louis XVI Restoring Liberty") as well as eighteen- and nineteenth-century Nantes designs—"Temple d'Amour" (1790) and "Les Miserables" (or "The Scottish Shepherds," 1815)—and some later nineteenth-century designs. The crispness of line is especially appealing to those who prefer the appearance of toiles as they would have looked in the eighteenth century when new.

Silkscreen painting on the wider modern cloth has largely replaced earlier techniques, while the eighteenth-century color palette has been enlarged from clear red, indigo blue, violet, sepia and aubergine to include pastels. The two-color technique used for some nineteenth-century toiles is employed in a wider range of color combinations for both eighteenth- and nineteenth-century designs.

Silkscreen printing is capable of yielding a variety of effects, from reproductions close to the originals to the softer outlines and colors on tinted grounds that simulate the appearance of antique examples. And the selection here is vast: most furnishing fabric companies and an increasing number of apparel fabric manufacturers offer toile patterns based to varying degrees on the originals as well as modern designs. Any category found in the plates is well represented. Genre scenes or pastorals—easily the largest group—include Huet's "Les Quatre Saisons" from Schumacher; "Vauxhall Gardens," an English design from Hinson; and "La Musardiere," a Manuel Canovas design through Cowtan & Tout. There is stag hunting, "Haywood" from Cowtan & Tout, and the English sport of fox hunting, "Hunt Party" from Scalamandre.

The popularity of chinoiserie is reflected in the number of varieties available, among them "Plaisirs d'Indochine" from Brunschwig & Fils, "Asia Toile" from Schumacher, and "Voyage en Chine" from Old World Weavers—all versions of a Jouy toile with scenes from Pillement engravings. Other chinoiserie toiles available are "Tisserand Toile" from Travers, and an English chinoiserie toile from the Bromley Hall printworks, called "Pillement Toile" from Scalamandre.

Other countries are represented by an 1816 version of "Monuments of Paris," printed in Munster, Germany, from Pierre Frey, and by "Dublin Toile," an early Irish design from Brunschwig & Fils.

Floral toiles exist in infinite variety, from realistic flowers arranged in graceful arcs of curving stems to the beguiling combinations of imaginary flowers and grasses typical of the Bromley Hall printworks in England. There are also toiles whose subjects fall into categories not represented in the plates herein—fishing scenes, famous nautical battles, scenes of domestic or exotic birds—and toiles of modern design in the manner of earlier styles ("Mount Vernon Plantation Toile" from Brunschwig & Fils). Resources in the United States, Canada, Great Britain and France begin on page 108.

The plates that follow are reproduced from *Toiles de Jouy*, originally published in the early nineteenth century. They are organized here by subject matter as follows: Country Scenes, Classical Themes & Mythology, Indienne Florals, Florals, and Woven Oriental Florals.

COUNTRY SCENES

1. Dove in an Arch

Blocked-printed in blue with minimal modeling, this simple yet pleasing design by an unknown artist was probably done in the early 1770s.

2. The Delights of the Four Seasons

One of the best-known and consistently popular toiles, this 1785 design by Jean-Baptiste Huet illustrates the seasons with scenes of a romanticized country life in which peasants and gentry mingle. Spring is represented by a maypole dance and gardening; summer, by scenes of the harvest, picnicking and fishing; autumn, by the picking of grapes for wine; and winter, by ice skating and driving in an elegant horse-drawn sleigh.

3. The Offering to Love

The scene for which this toile is named—an adolescent cupid, standing atop a low pedestal and being offered a lamb by a woman in classical dress—is set amid scenes of happy, bucolic childhood. Classical references, such as the ruins and the figures in antique dress, mingle with farm animals and figures in late-eighteenth-century garb. Jean-Baptiste Huet created the design in 1785 to reflect the romantic view of country life, an ideal popularized in the writings of Jean-Jacques Rousseau and taken up by the court of Marie Antoinette.

4. Rustic Vignettes

A collection of farm buildings is set within a frame of stylized trees and ornamented with flowers and birds. This block print from the mid-1770s is similar in style to Plate 1 and is perhaps by the same unknown artist.

5. The Gardeners

This multicolored block print is always referred to as "the Gardeners," even though only one man is surrounded by suitable equipment—spade, wheelbarrow, and watering can. The plate does not show fully the second figure, a woman in the large straw hat and shortened skirt of country dress, carrying a large basket and accompanied by chickens. Both figures are set within a sophisticated neoclassical frame of swagged drapery, garlands, and antique vases. The discovery of Herculaneum in 1711 and Pompeii in 1748 led to an increasing use of classical Roman decorative motifs throughout the eighteenth century, influencing this fabric produced in 1780.

6. The Activities of the Manufactory

This famous design, plate-printed in 1784 and the first of many by Jean-Baptiste Huet, was commissioned by Oberkampf to celebrate his factory's designation in 1783 as a "royal manufactory." Vignettes of the factory buildings (center, right) and the Chateau of Jouy (top left corner) appear, but of much greater interest are the scenes detailing the activities of the printworks.

Below the Chateau and to the right, a group of workers are beating bundles of wet cloth with flails to make the cloth as smooth as possible. To the right, with cloth laid on the table, the block-printer is pounding the printing block with a mallet to force the mordant into the cloth. Already printed and drying portions are draped behind him. Below, the plate-printer operates a press; the heavy plate is laid face up, and the cloth moves up and along as it is printed, while an assistant waits to reapply mordant. Neither printer is applying the actual colors of the finished cloth, but a mordant, which reacts in the dye bath to produce and fix the colors. The composition of the mordant is varied to produce different colors in the same bath.

After drying for several days, the mordant-printed cloth is soaked in a dung bath (below and left of the plate-printing scene) to dissolve excess mordant before being put into the dye bath of boiling madder, a Eurasian herb used for dying cloth red (top right). Another group of workers (right, near bottom) brush indigo onto the design, and to the left, workers are calendaring (pressing cloth between rollers to make it smooth and thinner) and polishing the printed cloth. The vignette at the top shows workers laying out lengths of cloth to bleach in the sun, which was done several times during production.

Oberkampf and his son Christopher appear in the design (center, at the bottom), and Huet is shown to their left, at his drawing board.

7. Hunting at Jouy

Descended from a family of artists, Horace Vernet was well known as a military painter of Napoleonic battle scenes. In his realistic portrayal of a stag hunt for this 1815 roller print, the figures are clothed in the manner of English hunting dress. The vignettes depict the landscape near the Bièvre River, with the façade of the Chateau of Jouy visible in the background to the left of the small building. A signpost above the resting stag is inscribed "Road to Jouy," "Vernet," and the name of the engraver, "Lemeunnie."

8. The Stag Hunt and the Boar Hunt

Before the French Revolution in 1789, stag and boar hunting were favorite occupations of the nobility and strictly forbidden to the lower classes of society. The generous repeat of the plate print affords an ideal ground for the widespread nature of a hunt and permits inclusion of typical views of landscape, rustic buildings, and vignettes, against which the excitement of the chase provides a unifying theme.

Although similar to many designs by Jean-Baptiste Huet, the precise date and artist of this design are unknown. It probably dates to the 1780s, and would have been among the early toiles produced at Jouy.

Unfortunately, this is not a full repeat—only the very top portion of the boar hunt is visible at the bottom.

9. The Fountain

This block-print from about 1770 depicts an elaborate, sculptural fountain framed by a somewhat haphazardly designed but very decorative arch, set amid roses and flowering trees.

CLASSICAL SCENES
& MYTHOLOGY

10. Cupids and Antique Scenes

This lighthearted design of cupids frolicking amid a profusion of neoclassical swags, volutes, and garlands was probably designed by Jean-Baptiste Huet around 1805. The finely engraved areas were roller-printed in violet and set off by a block-printed yellow ground. Except for the bust of Minerva, and a reference to Apollo in the lyre, the classical figures, flowers, and cameo-like profiles are treated as generalized classical decorative elements.

II. Medallions and Cartouches

Reflecting changes in taste during the Napoleonic period, Jean-Baptiste Huet's circa 1800–1805 design is a dense formal arrangement of references to Imperial Rome. Classical motifs and mythological figures—vases, the lyre of Apollo, harpies, the bull of Jupiter—are placed on alternately plain or patterned grounds and enclosed in lozenges or medallions framed in a classical manner by garlands and cornucopias. The short repeat is typical of a roller print.

12 & 13. Mythological Figures

Nineteenth-century toiles present a very different appearance from their predecessors, being typically more dense and symmetrical in arrangement, with a much shorter repeat. The classical influences of eighteenth-century designs—the airy, swagged garlands and drapery, the arabesques and volutes—have been replaced in this 1808 design by Jean-Baptiste Huet with precise rows of classical motifs arranged almost as though they were a collection of cameos. Lozenges and medallions hold mythological figures like the harpy

and representations of Roman deities—Minerva with her helmet and owl, and Venus and Cupid. These figures alternate with antique vases and portrait heads. All are framed and placed on a patterned ground.

The replacement of the cumbersome plate with an engraved metal roller permitted more rapid and continuous printing, but limited the repeat to the circumference of the roller, or roughly half the repeat of a typical eighteenth-century toile.

14. Diana the Huntress

Framed by vignettes of classical buildings now fallen into ruin and occupied by farm animals, the goddess Diana is shown in her incarnation as a huntress, armed with bow and arrow and accompanied by a hound. This 1802 roller print designed by Jean-Baptiste Huet blends the airy scenic qualities of eighteenth-century toile with a formally arranged band of cartouches enclosing symbolic animals and classical motifs.

15. The Lion in Love, or Leda

Known by a somewhat misleading title, this 1806 design by Jean-Baptiste Huet has three major scenes: a classically robed woman sacrificing a dove to Venus, a scene from the stories of Androcles and the lion, and the seduction of Leda with Jupiter in the guise of a swan (not seen in this plate). Divided into densely patterned geometric compartments, the overall design employs a vocabulary of classical decorative motifs to frame mythological figures and symbols such as the owl of Minerva and the eagle of Jupiter.

16. Lozenges

The background grid of lozenges encloses trophies of weapons, musical instruments, agricultural implements, cornucopias, the Imperial eagle and braziers—motifs familiar to eighteenth-century decoration but arranged here to reflect the taste of the Napoleonic era. A circular medallion encloses classically robed figures sacrificing at an altar adorned with the owl of Minerva, and alternates with a cartouche containing the goddess herself, with owl and serpent attributes. The cupids refer to Venus, the sheep to Apollo, and the grapevine-adorned goat to Bacchus. This circa 1800 plate print is less dense than subsequent toiles but still reflects the Napoleonic taste for formality and order.

17. Pompeian Motifs

Suspended against a lozenge-shaped grid with stylized foliage, Jean-Baptiste Huet's 1808
roller-print design depicts classical motifs enclosed in medallions and cartouches.
Portrait heads depending on ribbons from butterflies alternate with vignettes of cupids
and figures in Roman dress. Classical motifs had been familiar since the discovery of
Pompeii in 1748 and had become increasingly popular in French decorations as well as
clothing following the French Revolution.

18. The Four Elements

In a design of 1783–89 based on a series of late-seventeenth- to early-eighteenth-century engravings after L. de Boullongue the Younger, the elements are personified by Roman gods. Bacchus and Ceres in a chariot drawn by lions representing Earth alternate vertically with Nereids and Tritons cavorting in the waves symbolizing Water. To the right, Vulcan working his forge represents Fire, and Aeolus releasing the winds symbolizes Air. The scenes were set into cartouches separated by trophies and garlands in the neoclassical manner.

19 & 20. Monuments of Paris

Produced in 1818 after the death of Oberkampf, this is one of several well-known designs by Louis Hippoltye Le Bas (1782–1867). Four major architectural landmarks of Paris, each heavily framed and ornamented by trophies and classical figures, are formally arranged on a rosette-and-grid ground to create an imposing design. The monuments were carefully selected to symbolize the restoration of the French monarchy after the fall of Napoleon. To underline the importance, each structure is accompanied by a portrait medallion of the king who built it. In Plate 19 (left), the Fountain of the Innocents and

Henri II alternate with Perrault's colonnade of the Louvre built for Louis XIV. In Plate 20 (above), the Pantheon (or the church of Ste.-Genevieve) and Louis XV alternate vertically with the Pont-Neuf and Henri IV. A statue of Henri IV is in the foreground.

The two colors result from a combination of printing techniques: the red was roller-printed, and since the engraved rollers could not produce a solid area, the deep yellow ground was added by block-printing.

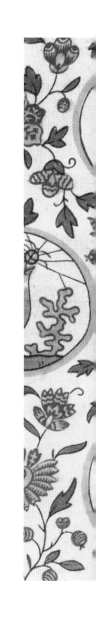

21. Chinese Motifs and Figures

A variety of naively rendered animals and two vaguely Chinese figures are arranged in medallions set on a ground of simplified flowers. The block-printed design probably dates back to the mid-1770s, when "chinoiserie" was in vogue. Depicting the figures as Chinese would have added to the allure of the design.

22. Floral

Incorporating realistic and imaginary flowers on delicate stems, this design was influenced by Chinese painted silks. The plate print is from the third quarter of the eighteenth century.

23. Persian Design

This well-known but misleadingly titled design contains vignettes of Chinese figures riding a water buffalo, crabbing, and playing a board game, then alternates with a scene of a decidedly exotic bird. The scenes are set within a densely leaved ground. The design was originally printed about 1780 at Jouy.

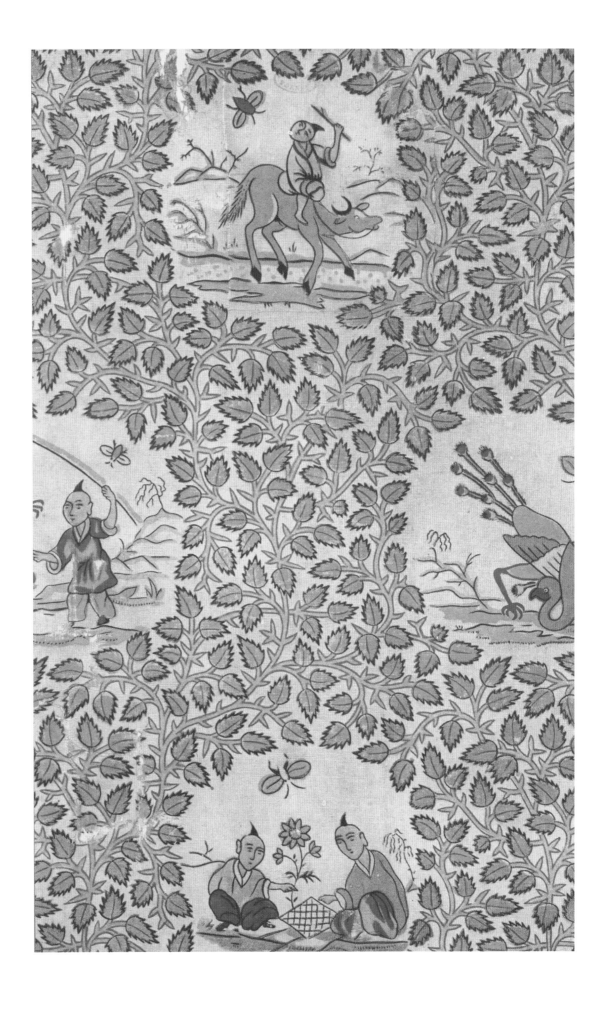

24. Oriental Vignettes and Lattice

The animals, birds and flowers in these vignettes are based on motifs used in hand-painted Chinese designs, as is the form of the lattice. Both the motifs and the lattice have been rendered in a more typically Western manner, with a certain naïve charm. The block-printed original dates to about 1775–1778.

25. Dianthus

Based on floral motifs typical of Chinese painted silks, this block-printed design from about 1775 includes the additional decorative element of a serpentine band of picotage (small dots of color) whose curling edges echo those of the flowers and leaves.

26. Chinese Vases and Flowers

Block-printed about 1780, this design of two groups of Chinese vases with flowers and fruits has been traced by Josette Brédif, author of *Printed French Fabrics: Toile de Jouy,* to its inspiration: a Chinese woodcut in the Boston Museum of Fine Arts.

INDIENNE FLORALS

27. Fantastic Creatures and Indienne Flowers

A circa 1775 block-print design blends imaginary animals and flowers derived from Indian chintzes.

28. Floral Rinceaux

Derived from Indian chintzes, this overall small-scale design of curving vines bearing stylized flowers was block-printed. In such a multicolored pattern, blue had to be added by hand, usually brushed on. And since there was no green in the eighteenth century, that color was made by combining blue and yellow. Close inspection of these two color areas will show a characteristic flow as from brush application.

29. Floral Trail with Ribbons

Delicate sprays of exotic flowers and fruits, tangled with fluttering ribbons, owe a debt to the work of Jean-Baptiste Pillement, who published several books of engravings of fantastic flowers and vignettes of Chinese life as he imagined it from travelers' reports. Both the floral and Chinese designs were widely influential from the time of their publication between 1755 and 1760, and became part of the decorative artists' vocabulary.

30. Floral Meander Border

This border is one of many produced at Jouy around 1775. It was intended for a variety of uses, such as trimming bed hangings, edging fabric wall panels, making tiebacks, or as a decorative band at the hem of a lady's gown or a gentleman's frock coat.

31. Flowering Branches

Block-printed about 1780, this design incorporates exotic Indian flowers on meandering branches, more typically Western in style, on a dotted tea-colored ground.

32. Indienne Floral with Birds

A block-printed design of exotic flowers derived from Indian chintzes.

33. Indienne Floral

Originally printed about 1780 in Jouy-en-Josas, the design blends realistic and Indian-style flowers on a serpentine stem resting on a ground of black picotage. The overprinted green is clearly visible.

34. Lozenge Floral

This block-printed Jouy design from about 1785 is characterized by stylized tulip-like flowers with patterned petals in the Indian manner, enclosed within a lattice of intertwined and patterned ribbon bands and set on a picotage ground. A similar version of this popular design was produced by the firm of J. P. Meillier et Cie at Beautiran, near Bordeaux.

35. Indienne Floral

A block-printed design of 1788 from Jouy displays a lush profusion of exotic flowers inspired by patterns on Indian chintzes.

36. Baskets of Flowers and Feathers

This late-eighteenth-century design with baskets of exotic flowers and feathers supported by undulating bands of intertwined ribbons is another illustration of the influence of Pillement's design.

37 & 38. Fruit and Flower Sprigs

Fruit and flower sprigs in this design were derived from Indian chintzes.

39. Floral

Even though this 1775 design is derived from Indian chintzes, the delicate, meandering stem with sparse flowers and leaves suggests the influence of the painted Chinese silks popular during the second half of the eighteenth century.

40. Indienne Floral

Block-printed design circa 1785 of exotic flowers derived from Indian chintzes was created by Monsieur Viry, a designer and engraver at the Oberkampf workshop. It was printed by the firm of Jacques de Maineville in Orleans between 1770 and 1790.

41. Lotus and Poppy Floral

Block-printed design of about 1775 in which realistically rendered lotuses, poppies and clove pinks are arranged in the manner of an indienne, with the spikey foliage typical of Indian florals.

42. Indienne Floral

In this block-printed design of about 1785, the clusters of exotic flowers are haloed on a ground of picotage. A very similar design was produced by the firm of Darnetal, near Rouen, about the same time.

43. Broken Sticks

A stylized indienne block print from about 1790–91 in which the typically graceful curved stems have been replaced by straight, stick-like ones that impart a very different rhythm to the design.

44. Arborescent Indienne

This block-printed design derived from the Indian Tree of Life patterns (or *palampores*) is adapted into a repeating design. Typically these patterns have a thick serpentine trunk bearing a wonderful variety of exotic flowers with patterned leaves and petals, mosses, trailing vines, and fruits. This type of design has remained popular since its first appearance and exists in a near-endless profusion. (Notes from the Musée de la Toile de Jouy date this 1780, while in a catalogue of the collection of the Bibliotèque Forney in Paris author Gilles Pitoiset dates it 1800 and attributes it to the firm of Hartmann Fils in Munster.)

FLORALS

45. Floral Sprays and Striped Ribbons

Realistic flowers and undulating bands of striped ribbon with scalloped and picot edges give this design a playful sophistication. In some eighteenth-century fabrics, the lack of green is due to the fading of the yellow, leaving only the very stable indigo blue; but in this case, the artist appears to have intended the leaves to be blue and violet. This fabric was produced by block-printing.

46. Floral Stripe

Red-and-black sprigs and sprays make a bold statement on a pinstriped ground. The limited number of colors suggests that this block print was an early design, possibly from the 1770s.

47. Floral Stripe with Meander

A block print in which sprigs alternate with a meandering flowering vine on a dotted ground called "picotage," which was produced by incorporating brass pins into the printing block.

48. Neoclassical Seat and Back

This plate shows a portion of a panel designed around 1818 to be used as upholstery for a chair: the large rosette was intended for the seat, the smaller rosette and foliage below for the box front (of the seat cushion), the smaller bar above (there would have been two of these) were for the arms. A second, smaller motif—not shown here—was for the back of the chair. The vertical pattern was for decorative bands, and the smaller rosette pattern at the base could have been used as filler. The panel was roller-printed and resist-dyed (see explanation with plate 60) in an indigo bath. The design is attributed to Lagrenee.

49. Ribbons and Roses

A veritable rose garden, this pattern of sprays enclosed within an irregular lattice of flow-
ered ribbon bands was probably block-printed around 1775.

50. Flower Sprigs with Vines

In this block print of about 1789, sprigs of mixed flowers are hedged with vines. The artist has used the overprinting of green (necessitated by the process needed to combine blue and yellow to make green, as there was no green dye available at this time) to his advantage, giving definition to the leaves.

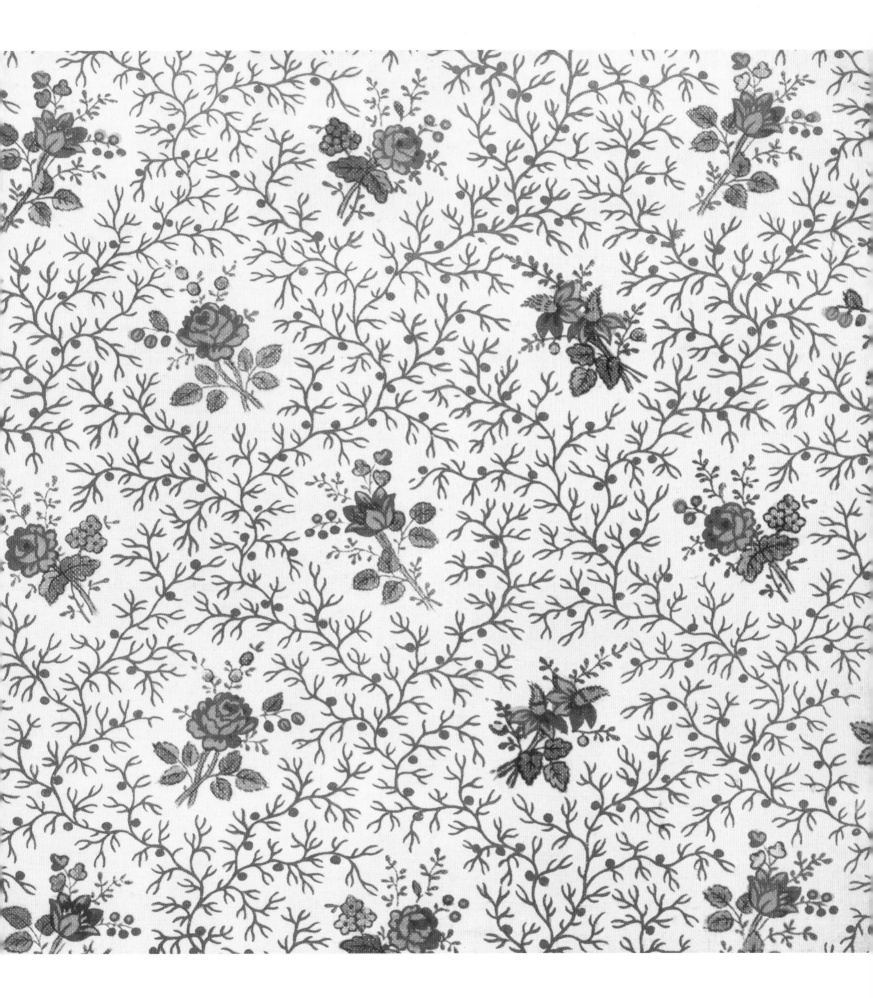

51. Flower Sprigs

The detail in the rendering of these realistic flowers in this late-eighteenth-century block-print suggests the influence of botanical drawings. The late eighteenth and early nineteenth centuries saw the publication of a number of important volumes of botanical illustrations, of which Rédouté's are perhaps the best known today.

52. Rose Sprigs Encircled by Myrtle

Printed around 1775, this pattern has rose sprigs in varied stages of bloom enclosed within garlands on an allover ground of dotted circles.

53. Scattered Flowers and Butterflies

Small floral sprigs are mixed with butterflies and a single caterpillar in this block-printed design from about 1780. Oberkampf had a dressing gown made from a similar design printed on a tan ground.

54. Ship Medallion and Bouquets

This sophisticated late-eighteenth-century block-print depicts a ship caught in a thunderstorm, set in a framed medallion adorned with a garland of flowers and ribbons. It alternates with a lavish bouquet on a ground of roses, separated by a narrow band with lilies on a fancy ground.

55. Floral Border

This is one of a variety of border patterns produced over the years by Jouy and used for trimming clothing, furniture, bed hangings, etc.

56. Dark Ground Floral

Known as *ramoneur,* or chimney sweep, for their dark, sooty-colored grounds, block prints like this were especially popular in the 1780s. Seen on a dark ground, usually the purplish-black known as aubergine or eggplant, the colors of the floral design stand out more brilliantly. Jouy produced a large number of this type; this example dates to about 1783–89.

57. Poppies on Picotage

Red poppy sprigs are haloed by black picotage on a dotted yellow ground patterned with picotage motifs to simulate a leopard skin.

58. Bouquets and Flowering Branches

Clusters of slightly simplified but realistic flowers are joined by flowering branches and trailing vines, outlined on a ground of red picotage with small butterflies. The join of the plate is clearly visible where the picotage overlaps.

WOVEN ORIENTAL FLORALS

59. Persian Floral Stripe

This pattern emulates a woven Asian fabric that was the inspiration for the design. Horizontal bars on the vine simulate the weave of the stylized flowers. The narrow-barred bands separating the floral stripes are printed to imitate those produced by a type of weaving called *cannelé*. This fabric was block-printed.

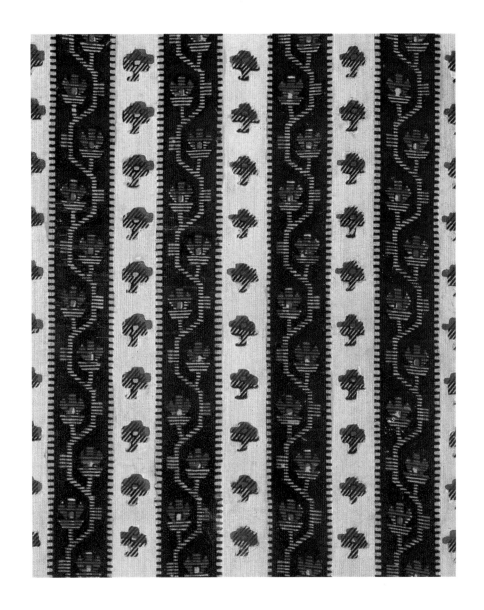

60. Stylized Feather Flower

In this resist block-print process, the colored and white areas were first painted with a paste resistant to the indigo dye bath, into which the cloth was then dipped. When the paste was removed, the white areas could be left plain or, as here, printed with an additional color. The feather-flower motif was inspired by exotic flowers portrayed in the woven fabrics of India.

61, 62, 63. Persian Flowers

The stylized oriental flowers on (a) and (b) were derived from woven fabrics, and were printed with diagonal bars to duplicate the appearance of woven designs. Small-scale patterns such as these were popular through the late eighteenth and into the early nineteenth centuries.

 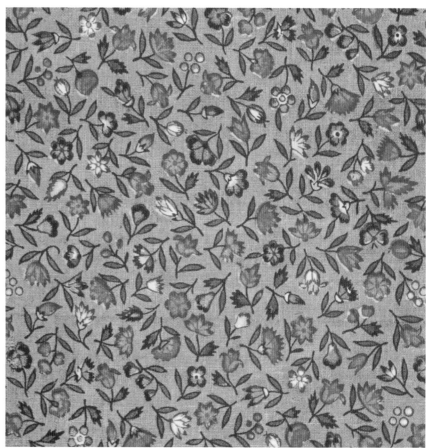

64. Indienne Floral

Above left, a design of about 1775 bears exotic flowers derived from Indian woven-fabric designs. This fabric was block-printed around 1775.

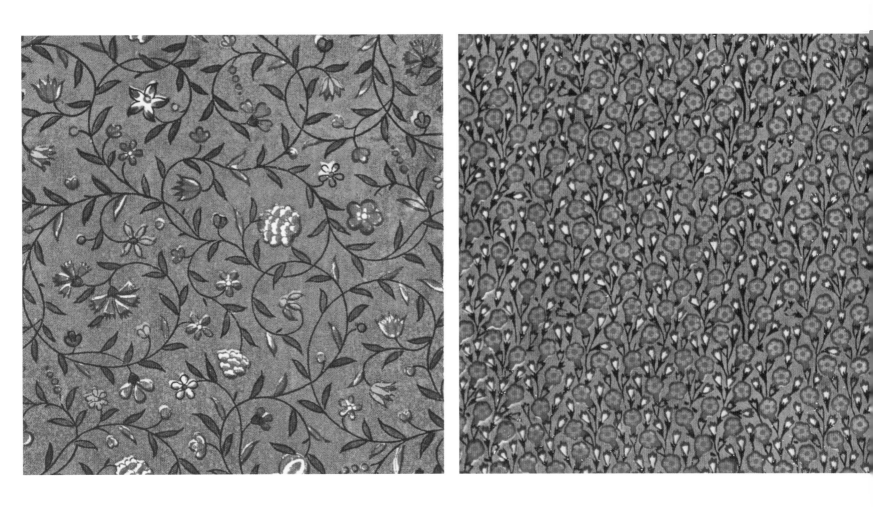

65, 66, 67. Stylized Florals

A sampling of stylized flowers, probably block-printed in the mid-1770s.

RESOURCES

The suppliers marked with an asterisk sell directly to the public through their shops or catalogs. The other companies listed sell only "to the trade," meaning that you will need to go through a professional designer, an architect, or the decorating department of a fine retail store to order fabrics from them.

*Ballard Designs
1670 Defoor Avenue, Atlanta, GA 30318-7528
404.352.8486, 800.367.2775

Patterns available:
  "Aqua Bird Toile"
  "Aqua Gazebo Toile"
  "Bird Toile"
  "Black Toile"
  "Garden Toile Blue"
  "Garden Toile Red"
  "Parchment Gazebo Toile"

Bastide Provencale
Office and Showroom:
2432 Brighton Place, Jeffersonton, VA 22724
703.328.8680
bienvenue@bastideprovencale.com
www.bastideprovencale.com

Blumenthal Print Works, Inc.
905 S. Broad Street, New Orleans, LA 70125
800.535.8590 USA, 800.654.4832 Canada
504.822.2147 fax
www.blumenthalprintworks.com

Brunschwig & Fils
979 Third Avenue, New York, NY 10022
212.838.7878
www.brunschwig.com

"Parc de Vincennes,"
photo courtesy of Brunschwig & Fils.

Patterns available:
FRENCH:
  "Bengali Cotton Print"—Long-tailed birds perched on curving stems. From a plate-printed cotton, Jouy, late eighteenth century.
  "Biscay Linen Print"—Diamond lattice formed of seaweed with shells and butterflies, enclosing floral sprigs. From a plate-printed cotton, ca. 1780.
  "Diana Cazadora Cotton Print"—Vignettes from the story of Diana and Acteon, whom she turned into a stag. From a plate-printed cotton, Nantes, ca. 1785.

"La Villageoise"—Vignettes of romanticized country life. From a plate-printed cotton designed by Jean-Baptiste Huet, Jouy, ca. 1785.

"Le Kakatoes Cotton Print"—Vignettes of rural peasant life and bourgeois domestic scenes. From a roller-printed cotton, Nantes, Favre, Petitpierre & Cie, ca. 1815.

"Les Sphinx Medaillons"—Medallions and pointed ovals with classical figures and putti, on ground with sphinxes, classical masks and frolicking dogs. From a roller-printed cotton designed by Jean-Baptiste Huet, Jouy, ca. 1810.

"Montalcino Cotton Print"—Two scenes of rural life. From a plate-printed cotton with additional color added by block, based on two wash studies by Dujardin, Alsace, Wesserling, ca. 1785.

"New Zinna Toile"—Floral stripe, from a plate-printed cotton, original printer unknown, late eighteenth century.

"Parc De Vincennes Cotton Print"—Vignettes of a zoological park with animals and figures. From a plate-printed cotton, Nantes, Favre, Petitpierre & Cie, ca. 1805.

"Pekin Cotton and Linen Print"—Chinoiserie toile with figures in an Oriental garden. From a plate-printed cotton designed by Jean-Baptiste Huet and his school. Jouy, 1780–1800.

"Plaisirs D'Indochine Cotton Print, or Cotton and Linen Print"—Chinoiserie scenes taken from Pillement's engravings of imagined Chinese life, framed by branches. From a plate-printed cotton, Jouy, 1780.

ENGLISH:

"Bird and Thistle Cotton Print"—Birds perched on serpentine stem with decorative grasses, ferns, etc. From a plate-printed cotton, Middlesex, Bromley Hall, 1780–85.

"Bromley Hall Toile"—Groups of cock and hen, or pair of ducks, framed by flowers and birds. From a plate-printed linen, Middlesex, Bromley Hall, ca. 1765.

"Chinoiserie à l'Americaine"—Scattered motifs of animals, birds, small buildings & flowers. From a plate-printed linen, probably English, late eighteenth century.

"Four Seasons Linen Print"—Four vignettes of the four seasons, framed by floral garlands. From a plate-printed linen, ca. 1770.

"Kininvie Cotton Print"—Birds & fruits framed by volutes and swagged draperies. From a plate-printed paper proof, 1780–90.

"West Indies Toile"—Botanical illustrations of varied palm trees in lattice of fantastic flowers. From a plate-printed cotton, probably Bromley Hall printworks at Middlesex, late eighteenth century.

IRISH:

"Dublin Toile"—Two vignettes of figures and stag with ruins, linked by garlands with fruit and bird. From a plate-printed linen, Ireland, Robinson of Ballsbridge, 1760.

LATER NINETEENTH-CENTURY TOILES:

"On Point Cotton Print"—Four vignettes of hunting dogs set in diamond lattice of branches. From a roller-printed cotton, French, mid-to-late nineteenth century.

"Sonnet 14 Toile"—Two scenes (gardening, shepherd & shepherdess) enclosed in floral lattice. From a machine-printed cotton, France, Rouen, Charles Besselievre, 1895.

MODERN TOILES:

"Gourmet Toile"—Vegetables. Modern artwork, printed to resemble engraved design.

"Mount Vernon Plantation Toile"—Vignettes of Mount Vernon and George Washington, with garlands. Modern artwork done in the manner of a late-eighteenth-century English toile.

BLOCK PRINTS:

"Creil Cotton Print"—Indienne flowers, plants and butterfly. From a block-printed cotton, France, Jouy, 1787.

"Herbier De Mister Peter Cotton Print"—Six different botanical floral sprays. From a block-printed cotton designed by Pierre Guillaume Lemeunnie (known as "Monsieur Pierre"), France, Jouy, 1787.

"Mevlana Cotton Print"—Indienne floral (same as shown in plate 35). From a block-printed cotton designed by Monsieur Viry, a designer and engraver at the Oberkampf workshop, printed in France, Orleans, by the firm of Jacques de Maineville, 1770–90. (See plate 40.)

Carleton V
979 Third Avenue, Suite 1532, New York, NY 10022
212.355.4525

Patterns available:

"Chiens"—Depicts a woodland scene of hounds flushing a covey of water fowl from a pond. Origin: France.

"La Chasse"—A classic toile, circa 1815 (Restoration), taken from a series of lithographs based on the works of Carle Vemet, who specialized in horses and hunt scenes.

"Tea and Sympathy"—Small vignettes with borders of flowering trees show some of the pastimes occupying the lives of oriental nobility. Origin: France.

"Toile"—Domestic tranquility is the theme of this toile, which shows graceful oriental figures in charming pavilions. Origins: Germany.

*Carol Brown
Putney, VT 05346
802.387.5875

Clarence House
211 East 58th Street, New York, NY 10022
212.752.2890, 212.755.3314 fax
info@clarencehouse.com
www.clarencehousefabrics.com

Patterns available:
BLOCK PRINTS:

"Chinoiserie Baroque"—Combines baroque and chinoiserie motifs of exuberant palm trees, garlands of beads and bubbles, and the court figures at leisure. From a 1795 document.

"La Marchande D'Amours"—Based on an 1817 toile de Jouy design of the same name by Oberkampf.

"La Plaisirs Chinois"—Reinterpreted from an eighteenth-century hand-painted silk. Offered in three colorways. (Same as plate 23.)

"La Vie En Chine"—A warp-printed silk depicting scenes of life in the Chinese countryside. The original eighteenth-century document was purple, printed on cotton, and covered the walls and a bed in a Lyonaise townhouse.

*Classic Revivals, Inc.
One Design Center Place, Suite 534, Boston, MA 02210
617.574.9030, 617.574.9027 fax
info@classicrevivals.com
www.classicrevivals.com
Representing Avigdor, Beaudesert and Borderline.

Patterns available:
AVIGDOR:

"Jaipur"—An early-nineteenth-century French design originally from a copper roller print, this toile depicts a large-scale bird roosting in the branches of an exotic tree.

"Toile de Jouy"—Originally a late-eighteenth-century copperplate print, this toile illustrates a typical overall floral vinous pattern.

BEAUDESERT:

"Amours et Medaillons"—Incorporates a netted background featuring delightful cherubs (Les Amours) carrying the traditional symbols of love. Designed by Jean-Baptiste Huet in 1805 for the original Oberkampf factory at Jouy-en-Josas.

BORDERLINE:

"Albertine"—Taken from an early-nineteenth-century French block print depicting period couples together in leafy rural bowers.

"Le Parc"—A large-scale pattern peopled with figures partaking in the pleasures of a mid-nineteenth-century park. Originally a block print.

"Serenade"—Originally a copper roller print, this toile depicts an early-nineteenth-century rural dance, a scene taken from a Watteau painting.

*Colorado Quilt

159, rue du Général de Gaulle
77230 Dammartin en Goële, France
33.164.02.71.65, 33.160.03.21.17 fax
www.coloradoquilt.com/eng/prod2.htm

Cowtan & Tout

979 Third Avenue, New York, NY 10022
212.753.4488, 212.593.1839 fax
Representing Colefax & Fowler, Jane Churchill and Manuel Canovas, and Cole & Sons.

PHOTO COURTESY OF COWTAN & TOUT.

Patterns available:

"Hispaniola"—Retraces the Battle of Trinquemale between British colonials and the West Asian Indians, in what is now Sri Lanka. Origin: France.

"La Musardiere"—Depicts scenes of country life: youths play together among trees, the harvest is reaped, and the freshness of the outdoors emanates from this fabric. Origin: France.

"Les Cavaliers"—Inspired by the Chinese painting *The Parse of the Emperor Xuande*, which dates from the fifteenth century (Ming Dynasty). Origin: France.

"Mandarin"—Traditional figures are present among Chinese architecture and oversized exotic floral life. Origin: France.

Also available:

"Animal Toile," Germany
"Chateau Toile," U.S.A.
"Chelsea Toile," England
"Chinese Toile," England
"Farnsworth," Switzerland
"Grosvenor Toile," England
"Harwood Toile," France
"Le Brun Toile," Switzerland

"Les Arts," France
"Lovers Toile," Switzerland
"Nambia Toile," France
"Virginia Toile," France
"Volagnes Toile," France

Decorators Walk

979 Third Avenue, New York, NY 10022
212.319.7100
Representing Lee Behren Silks, The Henrose Company, Henry Cassen, Peter Schneiders' Sons and Company, and J. H. Thorpe and Company.

Patterns available:

"American Independence" (Lee Behren Silks Ltd.)—Washington is shown guiding the chariot of Liberty, and Minerva is leading Franklin and Liberty toward the Temple of Fame. From a plate print, English, ca. 1785.

"Des Lanternes" (Lee Behren Silks Ltd.)—Scenes from a comedy after Rabelais called "Panurge dans l'ile des Lanternes." From a plate print, Petitpierre et Cie, French, Nantes, ca. 1785–90.

"Eighteenth-Century Scenic Toile" (J. H. Thorpe & Company)—Medallions with scenes of Washington, D.C., Philadelphia, and Mount Vernon, framed with flowers. (Also available in multicolor as "Eighteenth-Century Scenics.")

"Golden Toile" (Patterson-Paizza Inc.)—Elaborate toile with classical figures and a medallion of Ceres, accompanied by farm animals and peacocks. Huet, French, Jouy, ca. 1803.

"The Hunt Document Toile" (Oken Fabrics)—Scenes of early-nineteenth-century life and a boar hunt. From a roller print, French, early nineteenth century.

"La Gloire de Louis XVI" (Lee Behren Silks Ltd.)—Medallions with allegorical scenes signifying the love France bore for her king. From a plate print, Manufacture Gorgerat, French, 1789.

"La Pagoda" (Lee Behren Silks Ltd.)—Chinoiserie scenes, also known as "Pagoda on a Rock Bridge." From a plate print, French, Jouy, ca. 1775.

"La Plague de France II" (Lee Behren Silks Ltd.)—Medallions with pastoral scenes of shepherd and shepherdess framed by neoclassical urns, garlands, and classical figures. From a plate print, French, late eighteenth century.

"Le Chasse Coure" (Lee Behren Silks Ltd.)—Fox-hunting scenes. From a roller print, French, Nantes, ca. 1815.

"Le Chasse II" (Lee Behren Silks Ltd.)—Vignettes of stag hunting. From a plate print based on parts of a Jouy toile of stag and boar hunt, ca. 1783. (Same as plate 8.)

"Le Mouton Cheri" (Lee Behren Silks Ltd.)—Vignettes of elegant figures and peasants in country settings with ruins. Based on two lost paintings by Boucher. From a plate print, French, Nantes, ca. 1785.

"Les Chaveau" (Lee Behren Silks Ltd.)—Vignettes of elegant figures at a country picnic, and racing on horseback in an English park. From a plate print, Petitpierre et Cie, French, Nantes, ca. 1795.

"Marriage of Figaro" (Lee Behren Silks Ltd.)—Scenes from the play by Beaumarchais, with neoclassical motifs. From a plate print, French, Jouy, ca. 1785.

"Pastorale" (Lee Behren Silks Ltd.)—Also known as "The Offering to Love," this toile features country scenes and an altar to Love. From a plate print, Huet, French, Jouy, ca. 1795. (Same as plate 3.)

"Renaissance" (Lee Behren Silks Ltd.)—Vignettes of elegant figures and scenes of domestic animals, with volutes, in the late-eighteenth-century French style. ("La Grande Renaissance" is the same design rendered in a different style and on a larger scale.)

"Roxbury" (Lee Behren Silks Ltd.)—Lozenges with pastoral scenes framed by volutes and garlands. In the style of early-nineteenth-century French roller prints.

"Toile Ancienne" (Lee Behren Silks Ltd.)—Medallions and cartouches with classical figures linked by garlands on a patterned ground. In the style of early-nineteenth-century French roller prints.

"Toile Chinoise" (Lee Behren Silks Ltd.)—Chinoiserie vignettes framed by branches of fruit and flowers. From a plate print, French, late eighteenth century.

"Toile I" (Henrose)—Scenes of eighteenth-century country life, based on "American Liberty" by Huet. French, Jouy, 1783–89.

*Fabricland
Head Office:
2455 Highway 97
North Kelowna, BC V1X 4J2, Canada
250.860.6866
sew@fabriclandwest.com
www.fabriclandwest.com

Fonthill Ltd.
979 Third Avenue, New York, NY 10022
212.755.6700, 212.371.2358 fax
info@fonthill-ltd.com

Patterns available:

"Toile Vivienne"—A faithful reproduction of a nineteenth-century French toile originally printed with copper rollers.

"Turandot"—A traditional chinoiserie evoking the libretto of its namesake opera.

*French-Fabrics.com
7 rue de Bretagne
49230 Saint Crespin sur Moine, France
info@french-fabrics.com
www.french-fabrics.com

*The French Rendez-vous
9410 Montgomery Road, Cincinnati, OH 45242
877.937.3624 toll-free, 513.792.0252 local
welcome@frenchrendezvous.com
www.frenchrendezvous.com/index.htm

George N. Jackson Limited
Support Office and Manufacturing/Distribution Center
1139 McDermot Avenue
Winnipeg, MB R3E 0V2, Canada
204.786.3821, 204.788.2456 fax
www.jackson.ca

Greeff Fabrics
Schumacher Showroom:
D & D Building
979 Third Avenue, New York, NY 10022

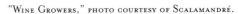

"WINE GROWERS," PHOTO COURTESY OF SCALAMANDRÉ.

Main Office:

200 Garden City Plaza, Garden City, NY 11530

800.223.0357

Representing Warners of London, E. C. Carter & Son, Inc.

www.fschumacher.com

Patterns available:

TOILES:

"Asian Toile"—Figures wearing turbans, lounging in a Chinese garden setting with vases and baskets of English flowers. Reproduced from a copperplate-printed toile, English, ca. 1805.

"Birds of Paradise"—A trailing branch design with exotic flowers and birds of paradise. Reproduced from a copperplate-printed toile believed to be French, ca. 1780.

"Danse Pastorale"—Genre scenes of country life in multicolors. Reproduced from a copperplate and woodblock-printed design by Dujardin, Wesserling, Upper Alsace, France, ca. 1785.

"Fruit Arbor Toile"—Clusters of fruit combine in a trailing branch pattern. Adapted from a copperplate-printed design, English or French, ca. 1800.

"Summer Garden"—An arborescent design with fruit and flowers. Adapted from a copperplate-printed toile designed by Joseph and Mary Ware, Crayford, Kent, England, ca. 1770.

BLOCK PRINTS:

"La Paradou"—Of a type of print known as indienne ordinaire, this design is of a ribbon and vine lattice with floral sprays. Adapted from a woodblock-printed cotton, Oberkampf à Jouy, France, ca. 1785.

"Pondicherry Vine"—A trailing vine pattern of leaves and flowers. Adapted from a mordant-printed and dyed chintz, India, ca. 1790.

"Ronsard"—Exotic stylized florals alternate with neoclassical stripes. Adapted from a woodblock-printed cotton, possibly by Petitpierre Frères a Nàntes, France, ca. 1785.

"Toulon"—A stylized floral and neoclassical motif alternate in vertical stripes. Adapted from a woodblock-printed cotton, believed from Mulhouse, ca. 1790.

Grey Watkins Ltd.

979 Third Avenue, New York, NY 10022

212.755.6700, 212.731.2358 fax

info@greywatkins.com

Patterns available:

"Amuse Bouches"—A classic pastoral farm scene rendered in a small scale.

"Enchanted Forest"—A tableaux inspired by an exhibition of eighteenth-century Portuguese porcelain at the Metropolitan Museum of Art. It recalls the influence of the Asian trade on European culture.

"Luberon"—A blue-and-white toile featuring medallions with scenic vignettes of Provence, a cozy garden niche, and a valley spanned by a romantic bridge.

"Scenes from Tuscany"—A lively pastoral scene emulating seventeenth-century decorative stenciling.

"Sungari"—An adaptation of a toile de Jouy upholstered on an eighteenth-century fire screen, found in 1996 at a Parisian flea market.

Hinson & Co.

Showroom:

D & D Building

979 Third Avenue, New York, NY 10022

212.688.7754

Office:

27–35 Jackson Avenue, Long Island City, NY 11101

718.482.1100

Patterns available:

"Arthemis"—Depicts the story of the Roman goddess Arthemis. Based on a nineteenth-century document. Produced in France, 2001.

"Belfort"—A contemporary French-designed floral tree of life, done in unusual color combinations such as teal and rust. Made in France, 2001.

"Blair House Toile"—A classic tree-of-life layout with floral motifs, done by an American artist after a sketch from the Hinson design studio. Made in the U.S., 1988.

"Canons Toile"—Baskets filled with fruit and flowers on speckled background. Contemporary design, made in the U.S.

"Eden Toile"—Another tree-of-life layout, but with fruit rather than floral motifs. This pattern was adapted and expanded from a nineteenth-century French hand-blocked wallpaper. Made in the U.S., 1990.

"La Campagna"—A classic pastoral design of peasants and farm life, taken from an old French document. Made in France, 2001.

"Mikado"—A classic French chinoiserie design, this nineteenth-century document has seen many incarnations. This version is produced in England, 2001.

"Ming"—Adaptations of this French design have been produced many times. Canovas Mandarin (this version), produced in France, is done in mostly bright contemporary color combinations. 2000.

"Mandarin" (this version) is done in mostly bright contemporary color combinations. Produced in France, 2000.

"Pastoral"—A classic country/farm/peasants scene from a French document. Made in England, 1999.

"Quainton"—An unusual toile of all boiserie and flowering shrubs surrounding a petit chateau. Based on a nineteenth-century French document. Produced in England, 1998.

"Vauxhall Gardens"—Lords and ladies enjoying themselves in the country. Redrawn from an eighteenth-century French document. Manufactured in England, 1996.

In the Beginning Fabrics

8201 Lake City Way NE, Seattle, WA 98115

206.523.8862

www.inthebeginningfabrics.com

J. Caldwell & Company

Janet Caldwell

1710 Camden Road, Charlotte, NC 28203

704.373.4098, 704.373.0241 fax

www.toiletoiletoile.com

Offers a variety of toile products such as personal accessories, home accessories, boxes, paper goods, and more.

J. Ennis Fabrics Ltd.

Head Office and Showroom

12122–68 Street

Edmonton, AB T5B 1R1, Canada

800.663.6647 English, 888.663.6647 French

780.479.6135 fax

support@jennisfabrics.com

www.jennisfabrics.com

*J. R. Burrows & Company

P.O. Box 522, Rockland, MA 02370

800.347.1795, 781.982.1812

781.982.1636 fax

merchant@burrows.com

www.burrows.com

*JoAnn Fabrics

www.joannfabrics.com

Kravet Fabrics

Showroom:

979 Third Avenue, New York, NY 10022

212.421.6363

Corporate Headquarters:

225 Central Avenue South, Bethpage, NY 11714

516.293.2000, 516.293.2737 fax

www.kravet.com

PHOTO COURTESY OF LEE JOFA INC.

Patterns available:

"China"—Chinoiserie vignettes. Modern, based on the eighteenth-century style.

"Garden"—Small vignettes of garden stairs or bridges set within an ogee floral trellis frame. Modern.

"House Party"—Scenes of country entertainment—picnic, dancing, bowling—in the eighteenth-century style.

"Lifestyle"—The same type of scenes are depicted on this toile as found on "House Party."

"Lila"—Scenes of gardening and of a shepherd and shepherdress, enclosed in floral lattices. French, Rouen, Charles Besselievre, 1895.

"O'Hara"—Pastoral scenes in the eighteenth-century style.

"Pasteur"—Figures in eighteenth-century dress are framed by dense foliage in the early-nineteenth-century style (1820–30).

"Pierre"—Vignettes of Italian life and monuments of Rome on a densely patterned ground. Also known as "The Roman," designed by Huet. French, Jouy, 1811.

"Richard"—Focus on floral designs.

"Sander"—Vignettes of animals in a zoological garden. Modern, in the eighteenth-century style.

"Scenic"—Vignettes of animals in a zoological garden. Modern, in the eighteenth-century style.

"Shadwell"—Chinoiserie scenes in a garden, in the eighteenth-century style.

"Shepherd"—Vignettes of elegantly dressed eighteenth-century figures picnicking by ruins in the country, in the eighteenth-century style.

"Squire"—Garden and chinoiserie scenes enclosed in a diamond lattice formed by a flowering vine, in the eighteenth-century style.

"Stanwick"—Large medallions of elaborate beds or chairs, set on a ground with smaller decorative motifs. Modern.

"Sumner"—Indienne flowers.

"Thaxton"—Vignette of a garden, with a basket of flowers, a hat, and birds, framed by trailing flowers, in the eighteenth-century style.

"Tobin"—Also known as "Homage of America to France," this scene shows America represented by Indians paying homage to a woman with a fleur de lys, who represents France. Designed by Huet. France, Jouy, 1783.

"Treilage"—Medallions of fanciful gazebos framed by garden implements. Modern.

"Trista"—Scenes of country life: picking grapes, herding ducks, and others, in the eighteenth-century style.

"Victoria"—Horse-racing scenes, including a depiction of Gladiateur—a horse who won the Derby at Epsom—and the Grand Prix de Paris in 1865, surrounded by figures in mid-nineteenth-century dress, with other scenes of racing along the sides. French, 1865.

"Wade"—Chinoiserie scenes.

"Warwick"—Vignettes of boys' games: bowling, badminton, jumping through a hoop, and spinning a top. From a plate print. England, Manchester, ca. 1770–80.

Lee Jofa Inc.

Showroom:

979 Third Avenue, New York, NY 10022

212.688.0444

Corporate Headquarters:

201 Central Avenue South, Bethpage, NY 11714

800.453.3563, 516.752.7600

www.leejofa.com

Patterns available:

"Allegorie a l'amour Toile"—Scenes pertaining to love in elaborate frames. A late-eighteenth-, early-nineteenth-century toile de Nantes, designed by Petitpierre.

"Boucher Stripe Print"—Taken from a small fragment found during the restoration of an eighteenth-century French bed.

"Four Seasons Toile"—A good example of the English toile style, depicting scenes of leisure activities relating to the four seasons.

"King George Toile"—English toile shows King George III and Queen Charlotte with their children. The Prince of Wales is shown on his horse. Windsor Castle is in the background. Late eighteenth century.

"La Chasse À Jouy Toile"—French toile depicts a hunt beside the Bièvre River, with the Grand Chateau of Jouy in the background. Designed by Horace Vernet and originally engraved in 1815. (Same as plate 7.)

"La Leçon De Danse"—A late-eighteenth-century toile in the chinoiserie fashion, this design was printed at Jouy but may have been English in origin.

"Robinson Crusoe"—English toile depicts scenes from the eighteenth-century novel by Daniel Defoe. Designed by F. Pieters and originally engraved in 1815.

Les Toiles de Jouy

24, Rue de la Libération

78350 Jouy-en-Josas, France

01.39.56.40.68

01.39.56.33.32 fax

www.toiledejouy.com.fr

Patterns available:

TOILES: (See Quadrille for descriptions)

"Ballon De Gonesse"

"Bonaparte"

"Chasse de Diane"

"Fête Navale"

"Fragonard"

"Greuze"

"La Bastille"

"Lafayette"

"Les 4 Saisons"—Villager scenes and varied games: the Vintage, the Harvest, the Fishing, the Bath, the Gardening, the Sledge. Jean-Baptiste Huet, about 1785. (Same as plate 2.)

"Les Pecheurs"

"Neptune"

"Nippone"—Incorporates oriental figures from comic opera. Fernan produced this composition from which only the hairstyles and the musical instrument could be said to justify the title. Jacques Fernan, late nineteenth century.

"Pillement"

"Robinson Crusoe"

"Temple d'Amour"

Marvic Textiles Ltd

Main Office:

1 Westpoint Trading Estate

Alliance Road

Action, London W3 0RA, England

011.44.20.8993.0191 sales, 011.44.20.8993.1484 fax

sales@marvictextiles.co.uk

U.K. Showroom:

Chelsea Harbour Design Centre

London SW10 0XE, England

011.44.20.7352.3119, 011.44.20.7352.3135 fax

U.S. Showroom:

Roger Arlington Inc

30–40 - 41st Avenue, 2nd Floor

Long Island City, NY 11101

800.960.1327, 718.472.9715

718.472.9713 fax

Patterns available:

LES TOILES ANCIENNES III:

A collection of classic toiles adapted from eighteenth- and nineteenth-century archive documents. All designs originated in the United Kingdom, except for "La Leçon," which originated in France.

PHOTO COURTESY OF F. SCHUMACHER AND COMPANY.

"Agapanthes"—The background architectural-style pattern of "Les Fables de la Fontaine," re-created as an all-over coordinate design.

"Aphrodite"—Figures of Aphrodite (goddess of love) and Artemis (goddess of hunting) surrounded by symbolic characters, animals, grapevines, and oak leaves on a finely patterned background. Designed for Oberkampf by Jean-Baptiste Huet at the turn of the nineteenth century.

"Eros"—Eros (son of Aphrodite) was created as a small-scale coordinate design, with medallions containing small details from Aphrodite printed on the same patterned ground.

"La Balançoire"—A traditional pastoral scene. Also available as a polyester/cotton voile that has a luxurious draping quality.

"La Bergere"—A romantic scene of a shepherdess and her beau in a charming rustic setting, and incorporating a textured background effect.

"La Leçon"—Depicts *une leçon agréable* of courting figures in a pastoral scene. The original was hand-printed in Jouy-en-Josas.

"MANDALAY BAY," PHOTO COURTESY OF OLD WORLD WEAVERS.

"L'âne"—A traditional pastoral depicting La Fontaine's fable, dating from 1806.

"Les Fables de la Fontaine"—A finely detailed, monochrome toile featuring eight fables written by Jean de la Fontaine, including "the two bulls and the frog," "the rat and the elephant," and "the lioness who has lost her cubs." Originally printed in Alsace in 1815, it has been adapted and recolored.

"Les Oiseaux"—Features groups of birds and trees in framed oval shapes that form a vertical stripe.

"Les Vues de Paris"— Vignettes of Parisian monuments, including the Pantheon, Louvre, Fountaine des Innocents, and the view from the Pont Neuf on a geometric background. Hippolyte Le Bas, 1818.

"Toile de Chine"—A detailed traditional Chinese illustration on a grand scale.

LES TOILES GALANTES:

A collection of pastoral-style, two-color toiles printed on a very fine 100-percent cotton cretonne base-cloth and woven in the Voges, as were these toiles in the eighteenth century. During the period, these versatile printed toiles were used as fashion fabrics and for furnishings. All patterns originated in France.

"La Fermette"—Simple country life portrayed in an intricate repeated panel framing a charming little farmhouse. Panels are interspersed with a small circular motif of a pair of nesting doves, and the whole design is brought together by intertwining floral garlands with a distressed ground. Eighteenth century.

"Le Galant"—A detailed design of palm fronds and roses around cartouches containing a scene of young lovers. Origin: France.

"Les Paysans"—The predominant circular motif depicts a peaceful scene of a traveling peasant couple with their donkey, surrounded in a contrast color by exotic flourishing blooms and placed at regular half-drop repeats on a subtle stipple-effect background.

"Les Romantiques"—A courting couple attended by their faithful dog is surrounded by lacy flower garlands. Reproduced with a distressed background to re-create the look of the original block-printed document.

"Toile de Velay"—Bold leafy florals divided and framed by a trellis. From an early nineteenth-century design from Ardèche.

"Vivarais"—An intricate repeated panel featuring a lovers' tryst, interspersed with bold floral designs. From an early-nineteenth-century design.

TOILES DE JOUY IV:

Five toiles de Jouy in a wide range of colors and designs, both classic and contemporary, to suit all settings—from the traditional to the more adventurous. All designs originated in the United Kingdom, except "Toile Carreaux," which originated in France.

"Empire"—Diana is depicted with her bow and arrow, running through a landscape with ruins and animals. A horizontal frieze of cartouches enclosing symbolic human and animal figures punctuates the pattern.

"La Chasse"—A vibrant and flowing landscape dominated by graceful trees and a stag-hunting scene. "La Chasse Voile" is the same design printed on voile that has a luxurious draping quality.

"Les Amours"—Cherubs on a background of hearts.

"Les Enfants"—Pastoral scenes of cattle and children, with classical details of ribbons and garlands on a detailed diamond-patterned background.

"Pompadour"—A one-color print featuring stylized pillars with sprigs of dainty flowers entwined about and trailing over them.

"Toile Carreaux"—A small-scale check available in colors that complement the Marvic toiles.

TOILES DE JOUY FABRICS & WALLPAPERS—

Finely detailed wallpaper reproductions have been carefully colored to coordinate with the following toiles:

"Aphrodite"

"Empire"

"La Chasse"

"Les Oiseaux"

"Les Vues de Paris"

"Toile de Chine"

LA VIE CHAMPÊTRE:

A collection of three toile designs, together with a large check in complementing colors. All designs originated in the United Kingdom, except "Damier," which originated in France.

"Damier"—A large, simple check primarily designed to coordinate with these new toiles.

"Les Sylphides"—This toile, adapted and recolored in our studio from a design produced in 1803 by Jean-Baptiste Huet, combines neoclassical style with pastoral elements. The motifs are printed in two tones on a contrasting textured trellis.

"Les Veneurs"—A traditional French hunting scene set near Rouen and depicted in finely drawn detail.

"Paradisiers"—A more modern version of a traditional toile, featuring exotic birds and butterflies with tropical plants and flowers, depicted in fine detail to closely resemble a copperplate etching from a botanical tome.

*MediaBoutique

8H30 a 20H30 du Lundi au Samedi
MEDIASBOUTIQUE—ECEP
BP701, 77017 Melun Cedex, France
33.64.87.56.00, 33.64.87.56.06 fax
mediasboutique@hfp.fr
store.europe.yahoo.com/elle-passions/r614.html

*Mitchell Fabrics

400 Spindale Street, Spindale, NC 28160
800.870.5312, 828.286.0227 fax
mitchell@mitchell-fabrics.com
www.mitchell-fabrics.com

Old World Weavers

D & D Building, 979 Third Avenue, 10th Floor
New York, NY 10022
212.355.7186, 212.593.0761 fax
www.old-world-weavers.com

Patterns available:

"La Dame du Lac"—Scenes from the novel *The Lady of the Lake* by Sir Walter Scott, published in 1810. Originally printed in the manufactury at Mulhouse, this copper-plate-printed toile typifies the Gothic revival style associated with the reign of Louis XVIII (1814–24).

"Offrande á l'Amour"—Ode to love and lovers, designed by Jean-Baptiste Huet, ca. 1785.

"Toile Nippon"—Inspired by a group of small eighteenth-century drawings depicting playful Oriental figures from Opera Comique. This toile, which turned out to be very Napoleon III in feeling, is still printed from its original roller. Conceived by Charles Burger during the latter part of the nineteenth century (ca. 1880–90).

"Voyage en Chine"—From the sketchbook of a late-eighteenth-century artist/observer recording impressions of his oriental odyssey.

*Pierre Deux

U.S. Corporate Headquarters
40 Enterprise Avenue, Secaucus, NJ 07094-2517
888.743.7732, 201.809.2500
201.319.0719 fax
www.pierredeux.com
Retail stores and showrooms throughout the U.S. Toiles de Jouy available in both fabric and matching wallcoverings. Contact for a list of available patterns and colors.

Pierre Frey, Inc.

Margaret McCutcheon
15 E. 32nd Street, 6th Floor, New York, NY 10016
212.213.3099, 212.213.3296 fax
www.pierrefrey.com

Patterns available:

"Fête d'Ete"—Chinoiserie amid large flowering plants. From a roller print, French, Jouy, early nineteenth century.

"La Colombe et l'Amour"—Cupids with classical motifs on a patterned ground. From a roller print, French, Jouy, early nineteenth century.

"La Dame du Lac"—Scenes from the poem by Sir Walter Scott. From a roller print, French, Nantes, ca. 1825.

"Le Petit Patre"—Vignettes of a young shepherd and friend framed by plants and trees. French, nineteenth century.

"Le Temps et l'Amour"—Medallions and cartouches of classic and mythological figures. Also known as "The Love Merchant." From a roller print designed by Hippolyte LeBas, French, Jouy, ca. 1816.

"Les Buvers"—Scenes of country life with peasants and the gentry. From a plate print, French, late eighteenth century.

"Les Muses et Le Lion"—Scenes of ruins with farm animals alternate with classical medallions. From a roller print, French, Jouy, early nineteenth century.

"Les Travaux de la Manufacture"—Scenes from the Huet design (plate 6) with color added. From a plate print, French, Jouy, 1783.

"L'Oiseleur"—Scenes of country life, on a plain or patterned background. From a roller print, French, late eighteenth/early nineteenth century.

"Mariage de Figaro"—Scenes from the Beaumarchais play, with neoclassical decorative motifs. From a plate print, French, Jouy, ca. 1785.

"Monuments d'Egypte"—Egyptian monuments and figures on a patterned ground. From a roller print designed by Huet, French, Jouy, ca. 1808.

"Monuments of Paris"—Major Parisian buildings on a patterned ground. From a roller print, German, Munster, Soehnee l'Aine & Cie, ca. 1816.

"Rejouissances Campagnardes"—Scenes of country life with elegantly dressed figures. From a plate print based on drawings by Dujardin, Alsace, Wesserling, ca. 1785.

"Scenes Champetres"—Scenes of romanticized country life, with medallions celebrating the Franco-American alliance. Also known as "American Liberty." From a plate print designed by Huet, French, Jouy, ca. 1783–89.

"3 Septembre 1782"—Episodes representing the French naval battle between the *Hero* and the *Superbe* on September 3, 1782, near Ceylon. From a plate print, French, Nantes, Petitpierre, 1783.

"Toile Villageoise"—Vignettes of romanticized country life. From a plate print designed by Huet, French, Jouy, ca. 1785.

Quadrille

979 Third Avenue, New York, NY 10022
212.753.2995, 212.826.3316

Patterns available:

TOILES:

"Ballon de Gonesse"—Depicts the flight of a hot-air balloon through the countryside. The balloon landed in Gonesse, where the townspeople attacked it as an alien object since they had never seen anything in flight such as this. Huet, Jouy, 1784.

"Bonaparte"—Glorifies Napoleon and his reign in several scenes: receiving the rulership of Egypt, attending the Assembly, and breaking the arrows of war to symbolize the Republic at peace. Nantes, ca. 1802.

"Chasse de Diane"—Depicts the goddess Diana with her bow and a wounded stag representing the demigod Acteon. Because he spied upon Diana when she was bathing, she turned him into a deer to be hunted and killed. Nantes, ca. 1785.

"Fête Navale"—Tells the story of Louis XVI's visit to Cherbourg to view the building of the sea wall. Petitpierre, Nantes, ca. 1786–87.

"Fragonard"—From designs by Boucher, this toile depicts rustic scenes of country life in eighteenth-century France. Petitpierre, Nantes, ca. 1785.

"Greuze"—Attributed to Greuze, this toile celebrates the festival of St. Catherine and the virtuous young ladies of each village and town. Jean-Baptiste Huet, Jouy, ca. 1785.

"La Bastille"—Started as a celebration of the reign of Louis XVI, this toile was modified during the French Revolution to depict the Restoration of Liberty and the image of the Bastille. Jean-Baptiste Huet, Jouy, ca. 1790.

"Lafayette," or "Homage d'Amerique"—Thomas Jefferson brought this toile with him on his return from Paris to use at Monticello. It depicts France's recognition of the new United States of America, represented by Indians in full headdress, blacks, and an émigré; the lady with the fleur de lys represents France. Jean Baptiste Huet and his school, Jouy, 1783.

"Les Pecheurs"—A ruin after the style of the Parisian painter Hubert Robert (1733–1808) is seen in this toile. The port features an interesting crane for stepping masts and two windmills, along with many other unusual details. Petitpierre, Nantes, ca. 1780.

"Neptune"—Composed of Neptune, Venus, and Cupid. Nantes, ca. 1788.

"Pillement"—A compilation of Pillement's favorite design motifs worked into an all-over diamond pattern. This toile, which was engraved for printing more than twenty years later, contains no fewer than eighty different motifs. Jean-Baptiste Pillement, Jouy, ca. 1787.

"Robinson Crusoe"—A newer toile from the end of the nineteenth century, this depicts images from the novel by Daniel Defoe, telling the tale of the shipwreck and solitary life of Robinson Crusoe. Burger, French, late nineteenth century.

"Temple d'Amour"—Inspired by a wall painting at Herculaneum, this toile uses classical motifs to express the images of love and happiness. Nantes, ca. 1790.

*Quilt Creations

7 rue de Bretagne
49230 Saint Crespin sur Moine, France
33.241.70.08.09, 33.241.70.08.88 fax
cecile@quiltcreations.com
www.quiltcreations.com

Scalamandré

Customer Relations and Distribution Center
300 Trade Zone Drive, Ronkonkoma, NY 11779
800.932.4361 toll-free, 631.467.8800 local
631.467.9448 fax
www.scalamandre.com

Patterns available:
BLOCK PRINTS:

"Carmen"—Small sprigs of exotic plants. Multi-colored block print, French, probably Jouy, late eighteenth century. (Similar to plate 37.)

"Revolutionary Toile," photo courtesy of Scalamandré.

TOILES:

"African Toile"—Vignettes with elephants, lions, giraffes, and other animals. Modern artwork.

"America Represented at the Altar of Liberty"—Another version of the "Revolutionary Toile" design, printed on narrower fabric with the figures slightly larger in scale. Plate print, English, ca. 1785. Special order only.

"Aphrodite"—Scenes of Aphrodite with cupids and attendants. English, ca. 1790. Special order only.

"Blue Mythology"—Medallion with scene of Telemachus and Calypso, taken from a Boucher painting, set among neoclassical motifs. Plate print, French, Nantes, ca. 1790.

"Bonaparte"—Multicolored, with scenes of Napoleon Bonaparte and allegorical figures. French, Nantes, ca. 1802.

"Cibelis"—Elaborate fountain with classical figures and a medallion of Ceres, accompanied by farm animals and peacocks. French, Jouy, designed by Huet, ca. 1803.

"Cupido"—Medallions with scenes of Eros, framed on a patterned ground. Roller print; French; Nantes, Favre, Petitpierre & Cie; ca. 1815.

"Don Quixote"—Scenes from the story of Don Quixote. Plate print, French, ca. 1785. Special order only.

"Fern & Thistle"—Features exotic and imaginary plants. English, Bromley Hall Printworks, ca. 1775–85.

"Hunt Party"—Fox-hunting scenes. Roller print, French, Nantes, ca. 1815.

"Italian Countryside," also known as "Occupations of the Farm"—Scenes of farm life. Plate print, Irish, ca. 1752–57. Special order only.

"Kenmore"—Swagged garlands of realistic flowers. Plate print, English, ca. 1765–75. Special order only.

"Pillemont Toile"—Chinoiserie figures in a rocky landscape with fantastic plants. Plate print, English, ca. 1760–75.

"Revolutionary Toile"—Washington and allegorical figures at the altar of Liberty, with portrait medallions of famous Americans. Plate print, English, ca. 1785.

"Tuileries de Jourdain"—Delicate floral with columns of interlaced vines and butterflies, in the manner of Pillement. French, late eighteenth century.

"Washington–Franklin"—Washington is shown guiding the chariot of Liberty, and Minerva is shown leading Franklin and Liberty toward the Temple of Fame. From a plate print, English, ca. 1785.

"Wine Growers"—Scene of grape pressing, framed by trailing vines. French, mid-nineteenth century.

F. Schumacher and Company

Showroom:

D & D Building

979 Third Avenue, New York, NY 10022

212.415.3900, 212.415.3907 fax

Main Office:

79 Madison Avenue, New York, NY 10016

212.213.7900

www.fschumacher.com

Patterns available:

BLOCK PRINTS:

"Pomegranate"—An arborescent chintz with peonies and pomegranates. Reproduced from a polychrome woodblock-printed cotton, English and French, ca. 1785.

TOILES:

"Carolina Toile"—Vignettes of romanticized country life are framed with scrolls, flowers, and fruit. Reproduced from a copperplate-printed document. English or French print, ca. 1780.

"Four Elements"—Classical mythological figures are grouped in scenes that represent the elements. Reproduced from a copperplate and woodblock-printed design attributed to Lagrenée, France, ca. 1785.

"Le Meunier et son fils et l'ande"—Illustrations for the story of "The Miller and His Son" from the *Fables of De La Fontaine.* Reproduced from a copperplate-printed design by Jean-Baptiste Huet, Oberkampf à Jouy, France, ca. 1806.

"Les Quatre Saisons"—Various scenes illustrate the activities of people and animals representing the four seasons. Printed in modern colors. Adapted from a copperplate-printed design by Huet, Oberkampf, à Jouy, France. (Same as plate 2.)

"Pleasures of the Farm"—Views of various rural activities of the late eighteenth century. Reproduced from a copperplate-printed toile, English, ca. 1785.

"Toile Orientals"—These oriental motifs are derived from an eighteenth-century book by Robert Sayer. Adapted from a copperplate-printed design, English, ca. 1775.

*Shabby Chic
310.394.1975
www.shabbychic.com

Stroheim & Romann, Inc.
Showroom:
155 East 56th Street, New York, NY 10022
212.486.1500, 212.980.1782 fax
Main Office:
3111 Thomason Avenue, Long Island City, NY 11101
718.706.7000, 718.361.0159 fax
www.stroheim.com

"LES TOILES IV: MERYVALE," PHOTO COURTESY OF
STROHEIM & ROMANN, INC.

Patterns available:

"Cathay Pavillion"—Features a charming chinoiserie design in a stripe layout hand-printed on pure silk, in three colorways.

"Country Squire"—Screen-printed on duck, this is a classic hunting scene in textured oval "frames" with traditional country motifs, colored in four somewhat masculine palettes.

"Meryvale"—Featuring country life motifs printed to give it a fine etched look, available in five colorways.

"Pastoral Symphony"—Based on a nineteenth-century document, this print combines widely spaced pastoral motifs with a highly textured and colored ground for a multilayered effect. Printed on a union cloth in five colorways.

"Plantation"—The pattern of lush exotic flowers and leaves is available in four colors on hand-printed silk.

"Summer Pleasures"—A traditional pastoral scenic available in both multicolored and monochromatic versions.

Summer Hill Ltd.
Showroom:
979 Third Avenue, Suite 532, New York, NY 10022
212.935.6376, 212.935.7957 fax
Office:
2682H Middlefield Road, Redwood City, CA 94068
650.363.2600, 650.363.2680 fax
Sales@SummerHill.com
www.summerhill.com

Patterns available:
TOILES

"Alfresco"—A toile depicting images of Italian country scenes, farms, horses, and hot-air balloons. Origin: Italy.

"Arabesque"—A French Rococo pattern of delicate arabesques, floral bouquets, and songbirds. Origin: U.S.A.

"Chan-toile"—A chinoiserie toile featuring cartouches of children at play, with vases of cherry blossoms, peonies, and chrysanthemums. Origin: Italy.

"Chelsea Gardens"—A gazebo surrounded by delicate garlands of fruit and flowers and gardening motifs.

"Filoli"—A painterly toile of garden vignettes, topiaries, and birdhouses. Origin: U.S.A.

"Four Seasons"—A toile depicting seasonal scenes of French provincial life, printed on gingham ground. Origin: U.S.A.

"CHAN-TOILE," PHOTO COURTESY OF SUMMER HILL LTD.

"Mariner Toile"—A classic seaside toile of light-houses, buoys, and fishing boats. Origin: U.S.A.

"Paradiso"—Playful chinoiserie fretwork follies with birds, Chinese courtiers, and foliage. Origin: France.

"Rosewarne"—Quaint sketches of Cotswald cottages in pastoral settings. Origin: U.S.A.

"Shangrila"—A whimsical block-print toile of willow trees, pagodas, and Chinese junks inspired by Cantonware. Origin: U.S.A.

Thibaut Wallcoverings

480 Frelinghuysen Avenue, Newark, NJ 07114
800.223.0704, 973.643.1118
973.643.3050 fax

Patterns available:

"Avignon"—This handsome toile features rustic mountain ranges, sportsmen on a hunting expedition, and stone laid castles. Based on a historical document.

"La Fontaine"—Tricolor document-based design depicting various scenes of provincial life.

"Portico"—Features small framed vignettes of women and children preparing a meal and cherubim leisurely lying about. Based on a nineteenth-century document created in Jouy, France.

"Rock Wood Toile"—Pastoral scene of women and men farming the land. Reproduction of an antique document.

"Toile de Frontier"—A document-inspired design featuring women, children, and various farm animals in a rural setting.

"Toile de Saison"—Features seasons of love and harvesting: a musician plays the flute as young couples dance and cherubim float above, a young couple courts as a chaperon looks on, villagers harvest wheat, and wine makers harvest grapes, crush them, and place the juices in skins for fermenting. Design is based upon a historical document.

Travers & Co. Inc.

979 Third Avenue, New York, NY 10022
212.888.7900

Patterns available:
TOILES:

"Bergere"—Elegant figures in pastoral settings. In the style of late-eighteenth-century French designs.

"Cumberland Hunt"—English hunt scene featuring the traditional horses and hounds. (Based on Horace Vernet's design shown in plate 7.) From a roller print, French, Jouy, 1815.

"Le Pecheur"—Multicolored design with pastoral fishing scenes. French, late eighteenth to early nineteenth century.

"Mythic Voyage"—Scene of Brittania in chariot drawn by lions, with chinoiserie figures nearby. From a roller print designed by Joseph Lockett, English, Manchester, 1810–15.

"Tisserand Toile"—Chinoiserie figures in the style of Pillement. In the style of late-eighteenth-century French toiles.

"Toile Venetienne"—Large-scale romantic toile featuring various scenes of Venice, gondolas, and costumed revelers. Modern design in the eighteenth-century style.

"Tree Squirrel"—Whimsical toile featuring cherubs and squirrels on a patterned ground. From a roller print designed by Jean-Baptiste Huet, French, Jouy, ca. 1806. (Similar to plate 10.)

Waverly Fabrics

Schumacher Showroom:

 979 Third Avenue, New York, NY 10022

Office:

 79 Madison Avenue, New York, NY 10016

 212.213.8100, 800.988.7775

 www.waverly.com

Patterns available:

BLOCK PRINTS:

 "Bengal Paisley"—Toile of a type known as Andrinople, usually exotic stylized flowers in rich colors, with red dominating. A modern adaptation of woodblock-printed cotton, France, ca. 1825.

 "Country House Toile"—Neoclassical design of floral garlands, rondels framing animal scenes, and symbols of country pastimes. A modern adaptation from a woodblock-printed cotton, France, ca. 1800.

 "Dominique"—A modern adaptation of a colorful print of imbricated scales, from a woodblock-printed multicolored cotton, Oberkampf à Jouy, France, ca. 1780.

 "La Petite Ferme"—Vignettes and symbols of farm life entertwined with garlands of flowers and vines. A modern adaptation of a copperplate- and woodblock-printed design, France, ca. 1800.

 "Mayenne"—Scenes of milling and playing children in a typical inexpensive print of the period. A modern adaptation from a woodblock-printed cotton, France, ca. 1790.

 "Rochelle"—Bright colors and familiar animal-and-plant motifs manufactured for export. A modern adaptation from a woodblock-printed chintz, of the type known as Portuguese Prints, France, ca. 1825.

*With Heart & Hand

258 Dedham Street

Norfolk, MA 02056

508.384.5740

*Zimman's

80 Market Street

Lynn, MA 01901

781.598.9432

www.zimmans.com

PHOTO COURTESY OF COWTAN & TOUT.

127